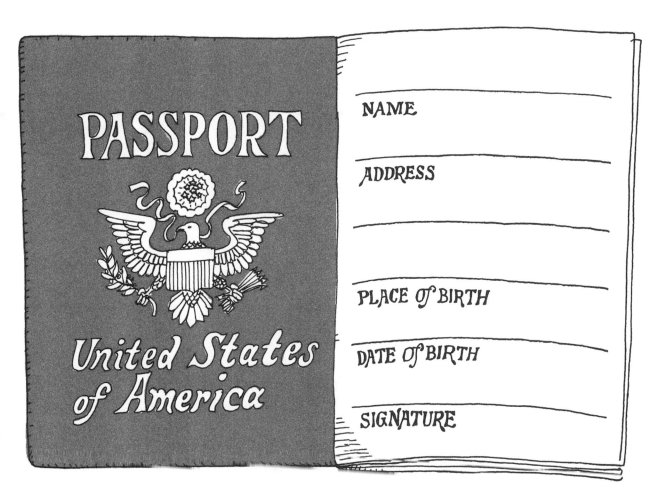

NAME

ADDRESS

PLACE OF BIRTH

DATE OF BIRTH

SIGNATURE

You are going to learn about the Land of Israel. Israel is a very special place for Jewish people. The best way to learn about a place is to visit. And we are going to take an imaginary trip to the Land of Israel. You will need a passport before we leave. Fill in the one above.

It takes a long time to fly to Israel.
This El Al plane is ready to land at Ben Gurion Airport.
Draw smiling faces in the windows.

You are always welcome in Israel.
It is your second home.
Cut out the letters and paste them in the house
in the correct order to spell ISRAEL.

The Land of Israel is very old. Jewish people have lived here for thousands of years. But the State of Israel is very young. It was born in the year 1948. We celebrate the State of Israel's birthday every year. Find out how old the State of Israel is. Write the numbers on the two candles and paste them on the cake. Then decorate Israel's birthday cake.

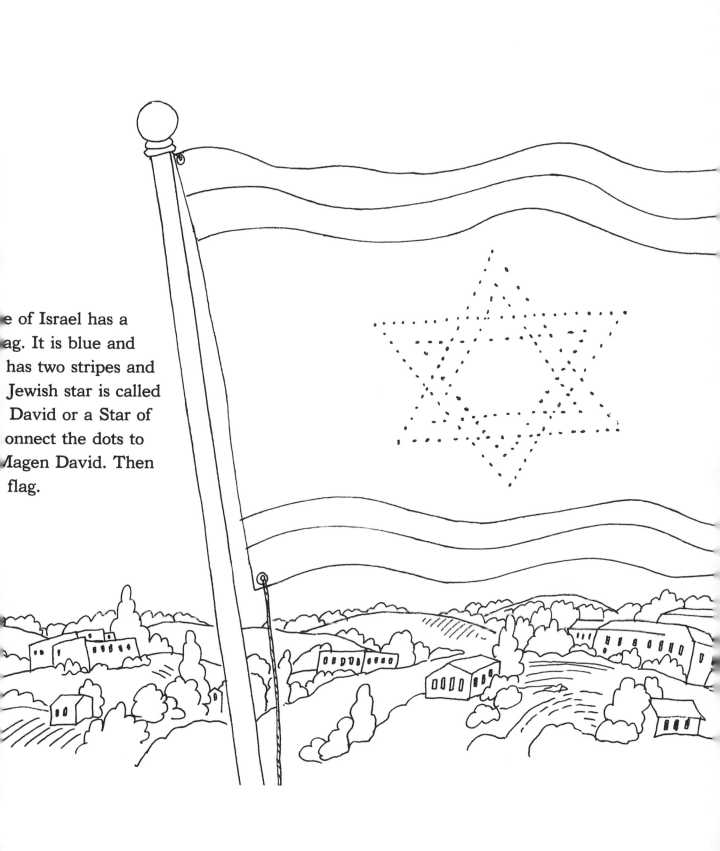

e of Israel has a
ag. It is blue and
has two stripes and
Jewish star is called
David or a Star of
onnect the dots to
Magen David. Then
flag.

There are five Hebrew letters hidden in the stained glass window. The letters spell the Hebrew name for Israel. Use a black crayon to color each space with a B. Use different crayons to color the rest of the spaces. Do you see the Hebrew letters?

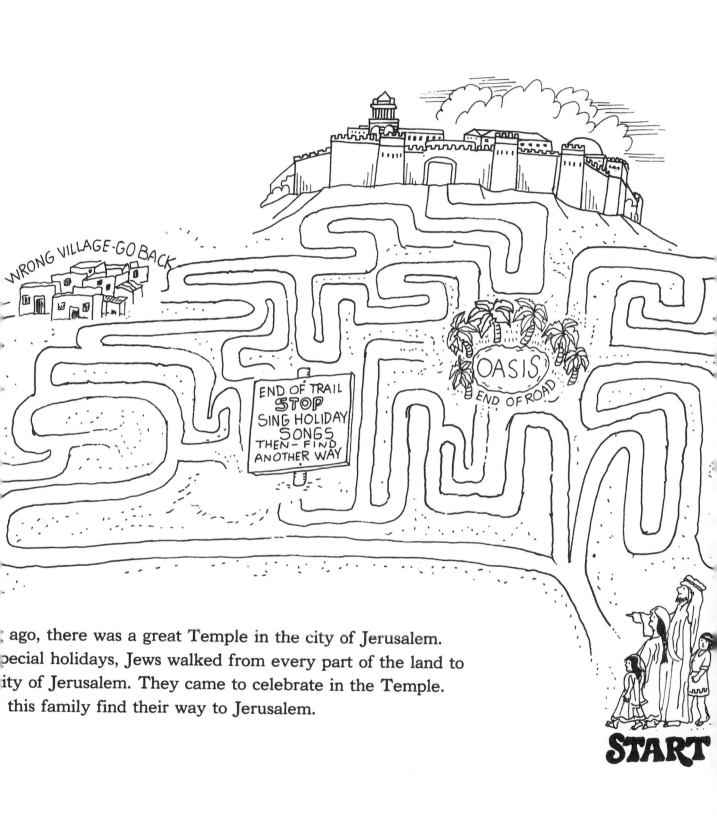

WRONG VILLAGE · GO BACK

END OF TRAIL
STOP
SING HOLIDAY
SONGS
THEN — FIND
ANOTHER WAY

OASIS
END OF ROAD

ago, there was a great Temple in the city of Jerusalem.
pecial holidays, Jews walked from every part of the land to
ity of Jerusalem. They came to celebrate in the Temple.
this family find their way to Jerusalem.

START

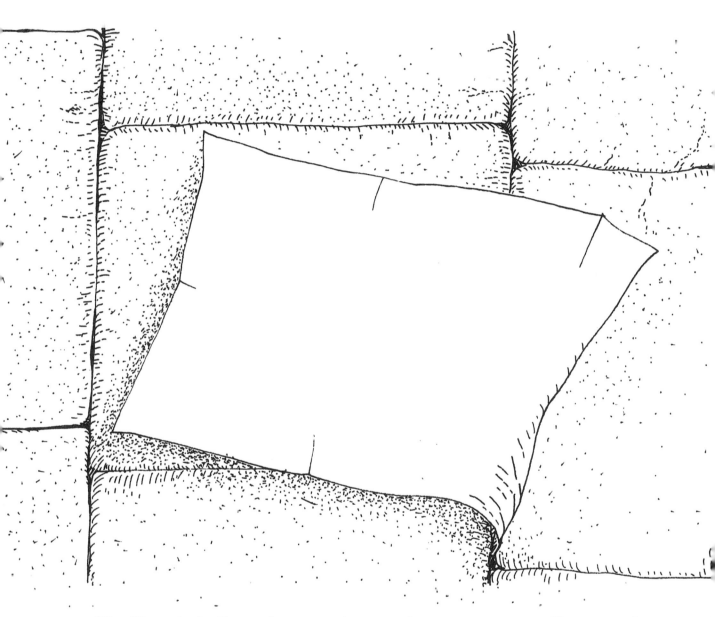

The Temple in Jerusalem was destroyed many years ago. But part of the stone wall around the Temple still stands today. It is called the Kotel. People write prayers to God on small pieces of paper to put between the stones in the Kotel. Draw or write your prayer on the paper.

Many places in the Old City of Jerusalem are important to Jewish people. There are places that are holy for Christians and Moslems too. We all share the city. It is important for everyone to be able to visit their special places. Help these three people become friends by joining their hands.

...tplace in Old
...s called the shuk.
...s line both sides of
...narrow streets. The
...ery busy and noisy
... is your shopping
...any things can you

...ING LIST
...OTS
...NGES
...WERS
...RELLA

...NS
...BREAD
...O BAG

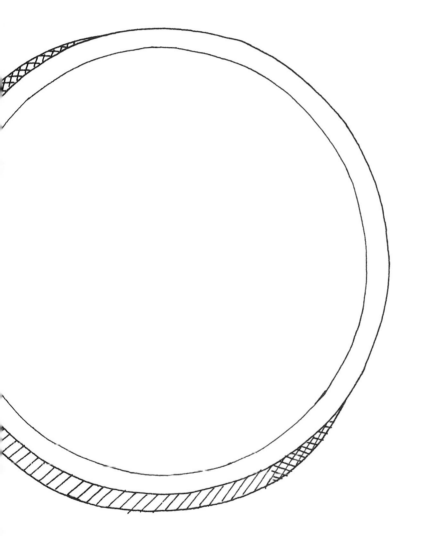

You will need Israeli money to b[uy]
things in Israel. One coin is calle[d]
a New Shekel. A picture of a pla[nt]
is on the coin. It reminds us of al[l]
the things that grow in Israel.
Other coins have pictures of plac[es]
and people. Can you design a ne[w]
coin?

Jerusalem is the capital of the State of Israel. The capital building is called the Knesset. Israel's leaders meet in the Knesset to make the country's laws. Can you think of three rules that would make your home a safer place?

LIST OF RULES

There are many wonderful museums in Jerusalem. One of the most interesting things to see is the Dead Sea Scrolls. A scroll is rolled up paper. Many scrolls were found in jars near the Dead Sea. Written on the scrolls were stories from the Bible and prayers. These words were written by hand many, many years ago. Some scrolls were torn.
Cut out the pieces. Can you put them together?

Hadassah Hospital is in Jerusalem. Here, Israel's sick people receive the care they need to get well. Twelve stained glass windows are in Hadassah Hospital. They were designed by the famous artist Marc Chagall. Each window reminds us of a Jewish family that lived long ago. This is the window of the family of Levi. Color the window.

1=black 2=red 3=yellow 4=green 5=blue

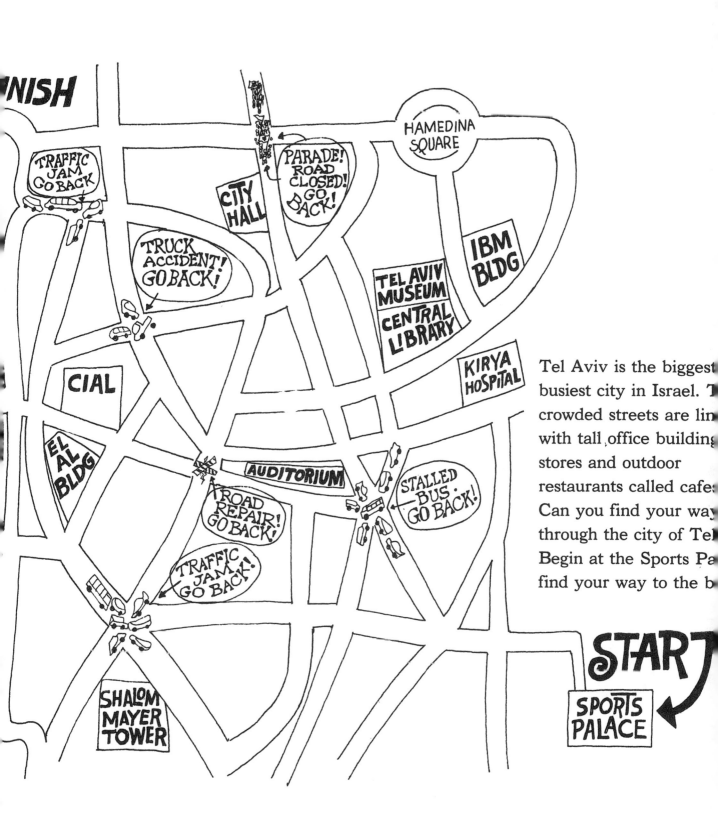

FINISH

TRAFFIC JAM GO BACK

CITY HALL

PARADE! ROAD CLOSED! GO BACK!

HAMEDINA SQUARE

TRUCK ACCIDENT! GO BACK!

IBM BLDG

TEL AVIV MUSEUM CENTRAL LIBRARY

CIAL

KIRYA HOSPITAL

EL AL BLDG

AUDITORIUM

ROAD REPAIR! GO BACK!

STALLED BUS GO BACK!

TRAFFIC JAM GO BACK!

SHALOM MAYER TOWER

START

SPORTS PALACE

Tel Aviv is the biggest
busiest city in Israel.
crowded streets are lin
with tall office building
stores and outdoor
restaurants called cafe
Can you find your way
through the city of Te
Begin at the Sports Pa
find your way to the b

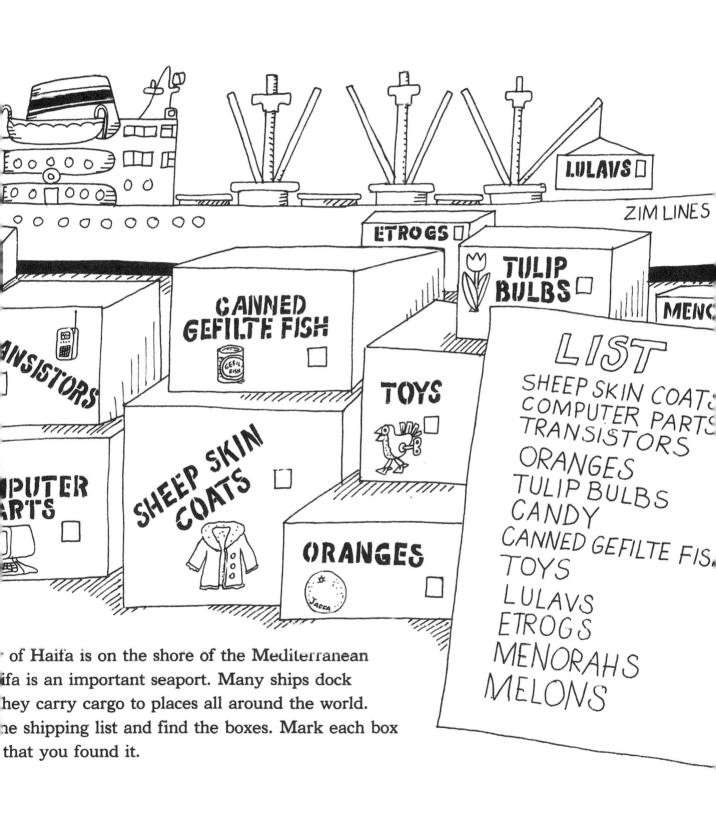

LULAVS □

ZIM LINES

ETROGS □

TULIP BULBS □

MENO...

CANNED GEFILTE FISH □

...ANSISTORS

TOYS □

SHEEP SKIN COATS □

...PUTER ...RTS □

ORANGES □

LIST
SHEEP SKIN COATS
COMPUTER PARTS
TRANSISTORS
ORANGES
TULIP BULBS
CANDY
CANNED GEFILTE FIS...
TOYS
LULAVS
ETROGS
MENORAHS
MELONS

...r of Haifa is on the shore of the Mediterranean
...ifa is an important seaport. Many ships dock
...hey carry cargo to places all around the world.
...he shipping list and find the boxes. Mark each box
...that you found it.

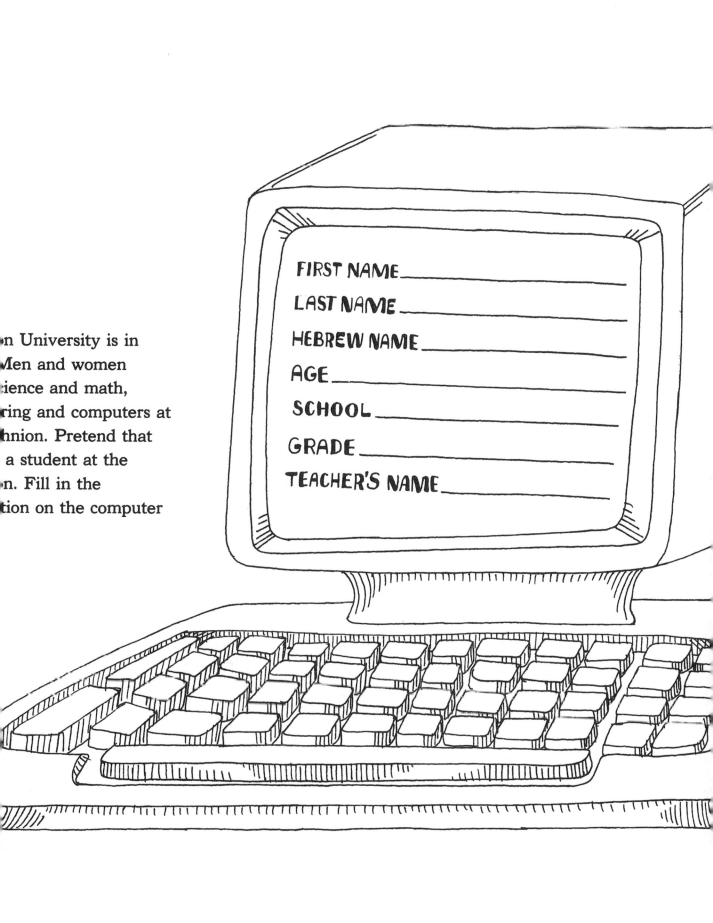

...n University is in
...Men and women
...ience and math,
...ring and computers at
...hnion. Pretend that
... a student at the
...n. Fill in the
...tion on the computer

FIRST NAME_____

LAST NAME_____

HEBREW NAME_____

AGE_____

SCHOOL_____

GRADE_____

TEACHER'S NAME_____

The city of Beer Sheva is very old. People lived there in Bible times! Long ago, Beer Sheva was a desert. The ground was very dry. Today, big pipes carry water to the thirsty soil. Now plants can grow in Beer Sheva. Add stems and leaves, fruits and vegetables to make the desert bloom.

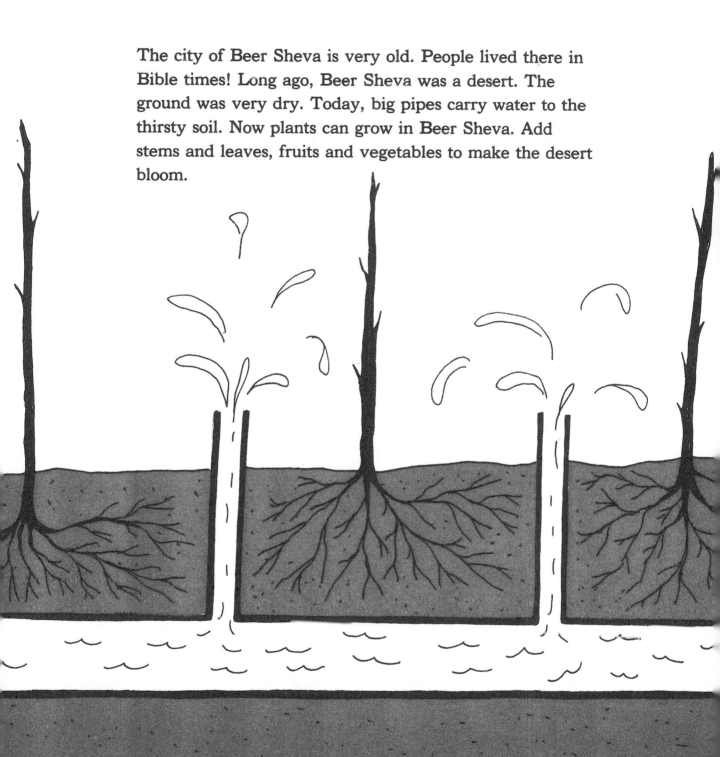

The city of Tsfat is in the mountains. At sunset, Tsfat is a very pretty place to be. Artists live and work in Tsfat. They paint pictures of this beautiful town. You can be an artist too. Color the picture of Tsfat.

Masada sits high on a mountaintop. A brave group of Jews came to this fortress long ago. You can reach the top of Masada in a cable car, but it's even better to hike on the winding path up the mountain. Can you find your way to the top?

START→

eople come to the city of Eilat on vacation. Here
swim in the clear blue waters of the Red Sea.
you can sail on a special boat with a glass bottom.
an exciting world to see under the water.
some fish to color.

In Israel, there are special villages called kibbutzim. People who live on a kibbutz get food, clothing and a place to live. Instead of paying for these things with money, grownups work on the kibbutz. Sometimes the children take care of the animals. Here are some animals for you to color and cut out.

ople called archaeologists dig in Israel. They find things
t help us know how people lived long ago. Here are
ne things the archaeologists found. Cut out the pieces
l paste them together.

A fruit called sabra grows on a cactus plant. From the outside, the sabra fruit looks like a small pear. Inside, the fruit is yellow and sweet. People born in Israel are also called sabras. Finish the picture of the sabra cactus by adding as many prickles as you can.

is the weather like where you live? In Israel it is
y hot and dry. Most of the children wear light,
er clothing all year long. Help this Israeli child get
for school.

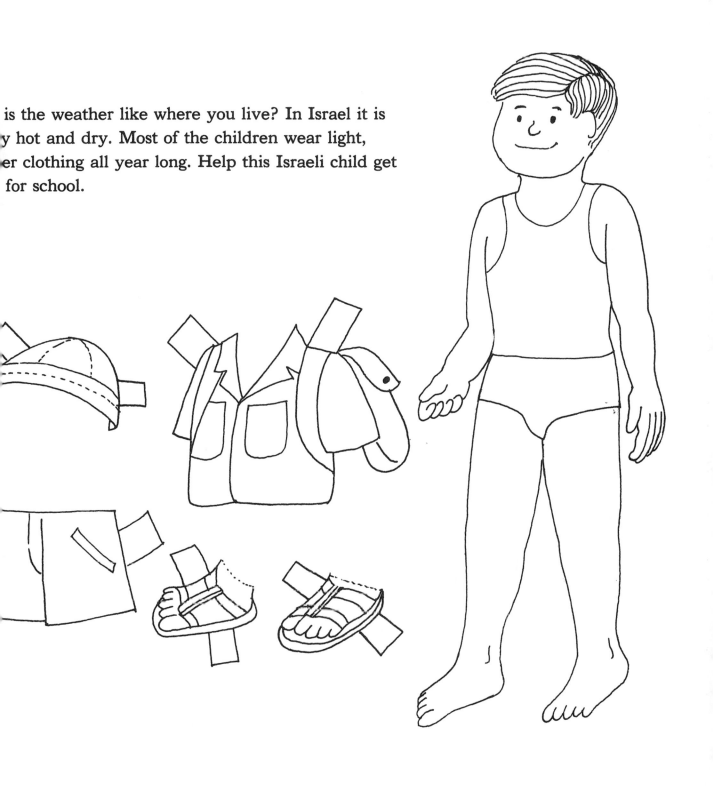

You live far away from the Land of Israel. But you can do something that will make you feel much closer. You can plant a tree there! You don't have to be in Israel to plant your tree. You can send money to the Jewish National Fund (JNF). They will use the money to plant a tree in Israel. You can help make Israel a much greener place. Color the JNF forest.

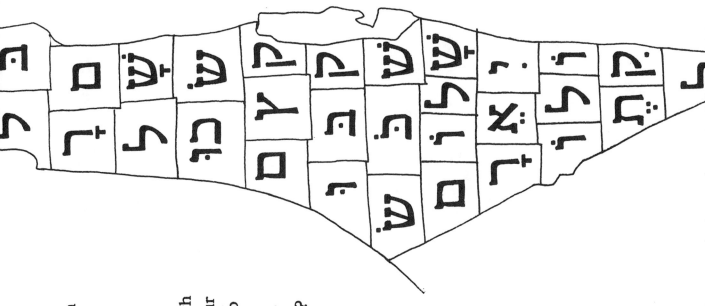

All people in Israel share something. In Jerusalem, in Tel Aviv, in Beer Sheva, in Haifa, in Eilat, and on a kibbutz—all people work and pray for peace (שָׁלוֹם). Peace means safety and getting along with neighbors. Every day, in our prayers, we ask God to help us bring peace to the Land of Israel. Can you find שָׁלוֹם hidden in the map of Israel?

In Israel, people speak Hebrew. Hebrew is a very old language. The Torah is written in Hebrew. You already know some Hebrew words. This book is about the Land of Israel (יִשְׂרָאֵל). You know the name of a special village—kibbutz (קִבּוּץ). You can shop in the shuk (שׁוּק). You can leave a prayer at the Kotel (כֹּתֶל).

We pray and work for peace (שָׁלוֹם).

Draw pictures to help you remember the Hebrew words.

MY HEBREW DICTIONARY

יִשְׂרָ
RAEL

שׁוּק
SHUK

כֹּתֶל
KOTEL

קִבּוּ
UTZ

שָׁלוֹם
PEACE

Many people worked very hard to build the State of Israel. They had dreams and they made their dreams come true. Theodor Herzl raised money to help build the country. Golda Meir made people see that Israel should be an independent Jewish State. David Ben Gurion helped build the first kibbutz. Henrietta Szold helped start Hadassah Hospital. Draw a picture of your dream for the State of Israel.

Each year, we celebrate Israel's birthday. Israel's birthday is called Yom Ha-Atzmaut. You can march in the Yom Ha-Atzmaut parade. Decorate the banner with words and pictures. Then color it so you can carry it proudly on Yom Ha-Atzmaut.

families move to Israel to make a new
in the land. Moving to Israel is called
g *aliyah*. *Aliyah* is the Hebrew word for
up." Can you go up to the Land of
Climb the ladder by answering the
ons.

at is in the middle of Israel's flag?
ich city is the biggest and busiest in Israel?
at do we call the wall that stood around
Temple?
at language is spoken in Israel?
ere do ships dock in Israel?
ere is the shuk located?

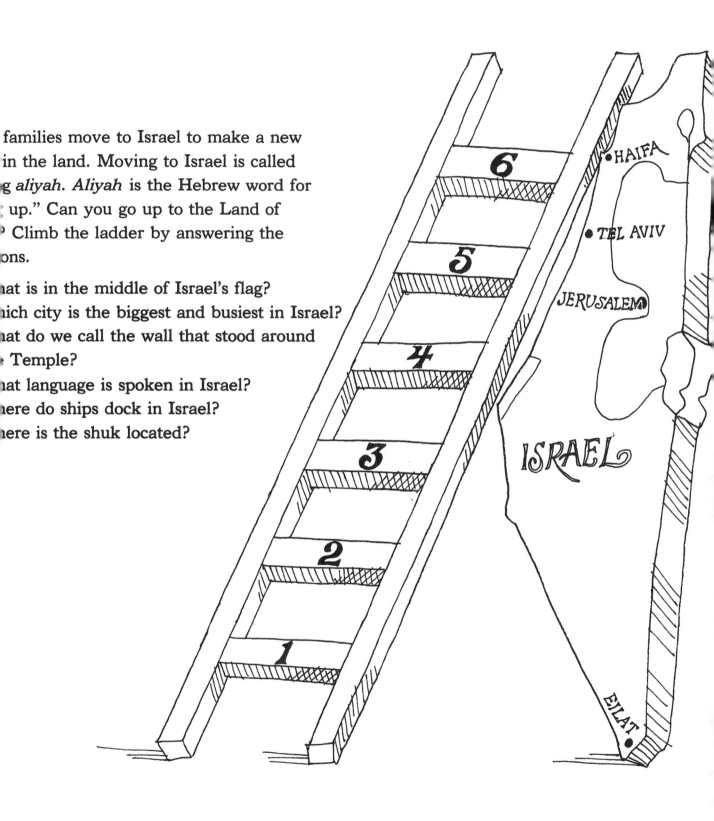

The State of Israel has its own special song called Hatikvah. Hatikvah is Israel's national anthem. Hatikvah is the Hebrew word for "the hope." The words in the song tell about the hope that Jewish people had for many years. We hoped that Israel would be a country where any Jewish person could live. We are happy that this dream is coming true. Can you learn to sing Hatikvah?

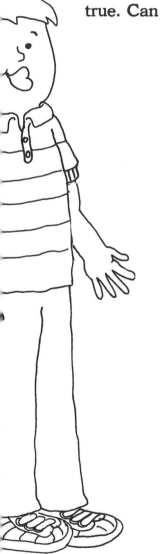

1 כָּל עוֹד בַּלֵבָב פְּנִימָה

Kol od ba-le-vav p'-ni-ma

2 נֶפֶשׁ יְהוּדִי הוֹמִיָה

ne-fesh y'-hu-di ho-mi-ya

3 וּלְפַאֲתֵי מִזְרָח קָדִימָה

ul-fa-te miz-rach ka-di-ma

4 עַיִן לְצִיוֹן צוֹפִיָה

a-yin l'tzi-yon tzo-fi-ya

5 עוֹד לֹא אָבְדָה תִּקְוָתֵנוּ

od lo av-da ti-ka-te-nu

6 הַתִּקְוָה שְׁנוֹת אַלְפַּיִם

ha-tik-va shnot al-pa-yim

7 לִהְיוֹת עַם חָפְשִׁי בְּאַרְצֵנוּ

li-yot am chof-shi b'-ar-tze-nu

8 אֶרֶץ צִיוֹן וִירוּשָׁלָיִם.

e-retz tzi-yon vi-ru-sha-la-yim.

www.ingramcontent.com/pod-product-compliance
Lightning Source LLC
Jackson TN
JSHW062201130125
77033JS00017B/594